101 HALLOWEEN JOKES

THE HENNESSY KIDS

THE HENNESSY ENTERTAINMENT COMPANY

101 Halloween Jokes / by The Hennessy Kids

ISBN 978-1-9994854-0-5 (Print)

ISBN 978-1-9994854-1-2 (E-book)

1. Halloween - Juvenile humour. 2. Wit and humor, Juvenile. I. The Hennessy Kids, author

The Hennessy Entertainment Company | HennessyEnt.com |

Copyright © 2022 by The Hennessy Entertainment Company

All rights reserved.

No part of this book may be reproduced in any form or by any electronic or mechanical means, including information storage and retrieval systems, without written permission from the author, except for the use of brief quotations in a book review.

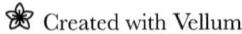 Created with Vellum

For Mom. Thank you.

1

SCARY EATING

What does a skeleton say before serving supper?
    Bone appétit.

What is a vampire's favourite fruit?
    A neck-tarine.

What do Italians eat on Halloween?
    Fettuccine afraido.

What is a monster's favourite food?
    Ghoul Guide cookies.

What kind of hot dog do you eat on Halloween?
    A Halloweenie.

What does a vampire never order at a restaurant?
    A stake sandwich.

What do you get when you're stuck between two witches at the beach?
    Sandwitched.

What is a vampire's favourite ice cream flavour?
    Vein-illa.

2
GHOSTS

What do ghosts use to wash their hair?
    Sham-boo.

Why are ghosts so bad at lying?
    Because you can see right through them.

Why do ghosts make good cheerleaders?
    Because they have a lot of spirit.

What is a ghost's favourite fruit?
    Boo-berries.

Where do ghosts buy their food?
    At the ghost-ery store.

. . .

What do ghosts drink when they're thirsty on Halloween?
    Ghoul-aid.

What does the papa ghost say to his family when he's driving?
    Fasten your sheet belts.

What do ghosts say when something is really neat?
    Ghoul.

What happens when a ghost gets lost in the fog?
    He is mist.

What is a ghost's favourite way to travel?
    By scareplane.

What tops off a ghost's ice cream sundae?
    Whipped scream.

What kind of makeup do ghosts wear?
    Mas-scare-a.

Where do ghosts mail their letters?
　　At the ghost office.

What are a ghost's favourite rides at the carnival?
　　The roller ghoster and the scary-go-round.

Who was the most famous ghost detective?
　　Sherlock Moans.

What kind of gum do ghosts chew?
　　Boo-boo Gum.

What kind of tie does a ghost wear to a formal party?
　　A boo-tie.

What's a ghost's favourite desert?
　　Boo-berry pie and ice scream.

When does a ghost have breakfast?
　　In the moaning.

What is a ghost's favourite party game?
　　Hide-and-go-shriek.

What kind of roads do ghosts haunt?
　　Dead ends.

What do ghosts drink at breakfast?
　　Coffee with scream and sugar.

Why do ghosts like to ride elevators?
　　It raises their spirits.

Where do baby ghosts go during the day?
　　Day-scare centres.

What is in a ghost's nose?
　　Boo-gers.

What did the boy ghost say to the girl ghost?
　　You are the most booooooooo-tiful thing I have ever seen.

What kind of shoes does a ghost wear?
　　Booooooooots.

What type of trees do ghosts like most?
　　Ceme-trees.

What did the ghost bring his ghost girlfriend?
    A boo-quet.

What kind of mistakes do ghosts make?
    Boo-boos.

Where do fashionable ghosts shop for sheets?
    Boo-tiques.

3

MONSTER MASH

Who are the werewolves' cousins?
    The whowolves , the whatwolves, and the whenwolves.

Where do most werewolves live?
    In Howl-lywood, California

What do you call a giant pumpkin?
    A plumpkin.

Why does a cemetery have to keep a fence around it?
    Because people are dying to get in.

Who did Frankenstein take to the dance?
    His ghoulfriend.

Why is Superman's costume so tight?
    Because he wears a size "S".

When is it bad luck to be followed by a black cat?
    When you're a mouse.

What did one owl say to the other owl?
    Happy Owl-ween.

Where did the goblin throw the football?
    Over the ghoul line.

Who is the messiest monster at suppertime?
    The goblin.

What do you get when you cross a black cat with a lemon?
    A sour-puss.

Why was the computer scary?
    It had a terrorbyte.

How do monsters tell their future?
    They read their horrorscope.

Why did the horseman from Sleepy Hollow go to business school?
    He wanted to get a head in life.

What do sea monsters eat for lunch?
    Fish and ships.

I want to be something really scary for Halloween this year so I'm dressing up as a tablet with its battery at 2%.

What do you do when a hundred zombies surround your house?
    Hope it's Halloween!

What do vegan zombies eat?
    GRAAAAAAAAINS.

Do zombies eat popcorn with their fingers?
    No, they eat the fingers separately.

What did the zombie give to his girlfriend for her birthday?
    Precious tombstone jewelry.

Why do you win the Halloween contest every year with your sandwich costume?
    I'm on a roll.

The maker of this product does not want it, the buyer does not use it, and the user does not see it. What is it?

A coffin.

Knock, knock.
> Who's there?
> Annie.
> Annie who?
> Annie body home?

Knock Knock
> Who's there?
> Ben.
> Ben who?
> Ben waiting for Halloween all year.

4

MUMMIES

What is a mummy's favourite type of music?
   Wrap.

Why was the mummy so tense?
   Because it was all wound up.

Why do mummies have so much trouble keeping friends?
   They're too wrapped up in themselves.

What do you call a mummy who eats cookies in bed?
   A crummy mummy.

Why don't mummies take vacations?
   They're afraid they'll relax and unwind.

Why can you trust a mummy with your secret?
   They can keep anything under wraps.

5
SKELETONS

Why didn't the skeleton want to go to school?
    His heart wasn't in it.

Why didn't the skeleton cross the road?
    He didn't have any guts.

Why did the other skeleton cross the road?
    To get to the body shop.

Why is a skeleton so mean?
    He doesn't have a heart.

Why don't skeletons ever feel insulted?
    Because nothing gets under their skin.

When does a skeleton laugh?
    When something tickles his funny bone

Who was the most famous skeleton detective?
    Sherlock Bones.

What do you give a skeleton for valentine's day?
    Bone-bones in a heart-shaped box.

Why did the skeleton stay out in the snow all night?
    He was a numb skull.

Why did the skeleton go to a **BBQ**?
    For the spare ribs.

Why was the skeleton a bad archer?
    Someone stole his bone and marrow.

Why did the skeleton go disco dancing?
    To see the boogie man.

Why was the boy afraid of a skeleton?
    Because it had a bone to pick with him.

How does a skeleton open his front door?
    With a skeleton key.

What musical instrument does a skeleton play?
    Trom-bone.

Why didn't the skeleton go to the Halloween party?
    Because he had no body to go with.

What do you call a skeleton that is always sleeping?
    Lazy bones.

How do skeletons travel in an emergency?
    In a skele-copter.

What instrument will you never see in a skeleton band?
    Organs.

Why did the skeleton love its ceramics class?
    He loved making skullptures.

What do you call a stupid skeleton?
    A bonehead.

What is the skeleton's funniest bone?
   Humerus.

What do skeletons use to text each other?
   A cell-bone.

6

VAMPIRES

Where do vampires keep their money?
    The blood bank.

Why did the vampire need mouthwash?
    Because he had bat breath.

What do vampires take when they are sick?
    Coffin drops.

What do you get when you cross a duck with a vampire?
    Count Quackula.

What do you get when you cross a snowman with a vampire?
    Frostbite.

Where does Count Dracula usually eat his lunch?
  At the casketeria.

Why didn't the vampire bite Taylor Swift?
  Because she had bad blood.

How many vampires are in this room?
  I don't know, I can't Count Draculas.

What is a vampire's favourite holiday?
  Fangs-giving.

What happened when the two vampires finally met?
  It was love at first bite.

Which building does Dracula visit in New York?
  The Vampire State Building.

What do you call a vampire without a girlfriend?
  A bat-chelor

What's it called when a vampire has trouble with his house?
  A grave problem.

What is a vampire's least favourite food?
   Stake.

How can you tell a vampire likes baseball?
   Every night he turns into a bat.

What songs does Dracula hate?
   "You Are My Sunshine" and "Sunshine on my Shoulder".

Why doesn't anybody like Dracula?
   He has a bat temper.

What has webbed feet, feathers, fangs and goes quack-quack?
   Count Duckula.

Why are vampires like dentures?
   They all come out at night.

Who does Dracula get letters from?
   His fang club.

Why did Dracula take cold medicine?
   To stop his coffin.

What type of dog does every vampire have?
    Bloodhound.

What is a vampire's favourite sport?
    Casketball.

What did you say when you knocked out Dracula in a feather pillow fight?
    Down for the count.

Which sports do vampires love to play?
    Bat-minton.

7
WITCHES

What is the most important subject a witch learns in school?
    Spelling.

What does a witch use to keep her hair up?
    Scare-spray.

What do you call a witch's garage?
    A broom closet.

What do you get when theres a witch in the desert?
    You get a sandwich.

What do witches get at hotels?
    Broom service.

What does a witch do on her birthday?
    She spell-abrates.

Why don't angry witches ride their brooms?
    They're afraid of flying off the handle.

What did the little witch want for her birthday?
    A haunted doll house.

How do you make a witch itch?
    Take away the W.

What do you get when a witch spins around a bunch of times?
    A dizzy spell.

Why does a witch ride a broom?
    Vacuum cleaners get stuck at the end of the cord.

What do you call two witches living together?
    Broommates.

What happens if you see twin witches?
    You won't be able to see which witch is which.

Why did the witch give up fortune telling?
>   There was no future in it.

What is a witch with poison ivy called?
>   An itchy witchy.

What's a cold, evil candle called?
>   The wicked wick of the north.

Why do all the witches like to wander on brooms?
>   Because the vacuum cleaners are too expensive for them.

How does a witch tell time?
>   She looks at her witch watch.

Who turns off the lights on Halloween?
>   The lights witch.

8
YOUR FAVOURITE JOKE

What is your favourite Halloween joke that isn't in this book?

Send it to us at thehennessykids@gmail.com, and we'll look to share it online with all our friends.

ACKNOWLEDGMENTS

A lot of people in our family listen to our jokes, so we want to say thank you to Aunt Barbara, Aunt Carol, Aunt Lisa, Aunt Rhonda, Uncle Scott, Uncle Stephen, Uncle Timothy, and Grammie and Grampie.

ABOUT THE AUTHORS

The Hennessy Kids think the world would be better with more smiles.

Want to know when our new books are available? Sign up for our **Fun Stuff With Heart** newsletter at HennessyEnt.com.

BOOKS BY THE HENNESSY KIDS

101 Halloween Jokes

101 Christmas Jokes

101 Pet Jokes

101 Knock Knock Jokes, Vol. 1

101 Nature Jokes

101 Food Jokes

www.ingramcontent.com/pod-product-compliance
Lightning Source LLC
Chambersburg PA
CBHW052127070526
44586CB00016B/2118